Exploring the Great Basin

Samuel Voz

INFOMAX COMMON CORE READERS

Rosen Classroom™

New York

Published in 2014 by The Rosen Publishing Group, Inc.
29 East 21st Street, New York, NY 10010

Book Design: Jon D'Rozario

Photo Credits: Cover Jeffrey M. Frank/Shutterstock.com; pp. 3, 4, 6, 8, 10, 12, 14, 16, 18, 20, 22, 23, 24 (background)
Jason Patrick Ross/Shutterstock.com; p. 5 (map) Dr_Flash/Shutterstock.com; p. 5 (desert) Johnny Adolphson/
Shutterstock.com; p. 7 Galyna Andrushko/Shutterstock.com; p. 9 Joy Stein/Shutterstock.com; p. 11 Zack Frank/
Shutterstock.com; p. 13 Brendan Bucy/Shutterstock.com; pp. 15, 21 Matt Jeppson/Shutterstock.com; p. 17 mlorenz/
Shutterstock.com; p. 19 Nate Allred/Shutterstock.com; p. 22 (mountain lion) CatonPhoto/Shutterstock.com; p. 22 (coyote)
kojihirano/Shutterstock.com; p. 22 (badger) Max Allen/Shutterstock.com; p. 22 (sheep) 9174577312/Shutterstock.com.

ISBN: 978-1-4777-2491-0
6-pack ISBN: 978-1-4777-2492-7

Manufactured in the United States of America

CPSIA Compliance Information: Batch #CS13RC: For further information contact Rosen Publishing, New York, New York at 1-800-237-9932.

Contents

The Largest U.S. Desert   4

Plants in the Desert   8

The Great Basin Rattlesnake   14

Birds and Bugs   16

Lots of Lizards!   20

Mammals of the Great Basin Desert   22

Glossary   23

Index   24

The Largest U.S. Desert

The Great Basin is a large **region** in the western United States known for its dry land. The most famous part of the Great Basin is the Great Basin Desert. This desert is 190,000 square miles (492,000 sq km) in size and runs through several states, including Nevada, Idaho, California, Utah, and Oregon. The Great Basin Desert is the largest desert in the United States!

The explorer John C. Frémont gave the Great Basin its name. He traveled through this region between 1843 and 1845.

The Great Basin Desert is one of four North American deserts. The other three are the Sonoran (suh-NOHR-uhn), Chihuahuan (chee-WAH-wahn), and Mojave (moh-HAH-vee).

Great Basin

The Great Basin Desert sits between two mountain ranges, or groups of mountains. The Sierra Nevada are to the west, and the Rocky Mountains are to the east. They give this region its dry, cool weather.

The Sierra Nevada keep rain from reaching the Great Basin Desert because they're so tall. Only 6 to 12 inches (15 to 30 cm) of **precipitation** fall in the Great Basin Desert each year. The height of the Great Basin creates a cold desert **environment**. It snows in some parts of the region.

Some mountains in the Great Basin are over 9,000 feet (2,740 m) tall!

Plants in the Desert

The plants in the Great Basin Desert have **adapted** over time to life in this rocky desert. They've found ways to get water even in the driest weather and hold on to it for a long time.

The Great Basin bristlecone pine is one kind of tree found in this region. It's the world's longest-living tree, and it can live for almost 5,000 years! These trees grow slowly and can grow in very rocky soil. This makes them well suited for the desert.

The Great Basin bristlecone pine is a kind of tree that lives longest when the conditions for growing are the toughest.

Many other kinds of trees have also adapted to life in the Great Basin Desert. Limber pine trees can live almost as long as the Great Basin bristlecone pine—3,000 years! Douglas fir is a kind of tree with wood that's highly valued in the West.

Many smaller plants make their homes in the Great Basin Desert, too. Shrubs are found throughout the region. These short, woody plants have many stems.

The leaves on many plants in the Great Basin Desert are waxy, which allows them to hold onto water in even the driest weather.

Big sagebrush is one of the most common plants in the Great Basin Desert. It has many features that help it grow in the region's dry soil. Big sagebrush has gray and green leaves that are hairy. The hairy leaves keep water in the plant even when it's windy.

The roots of a big sagebrush plant grow far into the soil. They can reach up to 90 feet (27 m) around the plant in a circle! Then, the plant can get as much water as possible.

In August, yellow flowers appear on big sagebrush plants.

The Great Basin Rattlesnake

The animals that live in the Great Basin Desert have also adapted to desert life over the years. The Great Basin rattlesnake is one of these animals. It's light brown or gray, which helps it blend in with the sand and rocks as it waits for its prey. These snakes eat small **mammals**, birds, lizards, and many other kinds of animals.

First, the Great Basin rattlesnake bites its prey with its sharp teeth, or fangs. Then, the **venom** in the fangs kills the animal.

After the Great Basin rattlesnake kills its prey, it swallows the animal whole!

Birds and Bugs

The Great Basin rattlesnake's main predators are hawks and other hunting birds. There are many other kinds of birds in the skies above the Great Basin, too. This region is home to blackbirds and sparrows. It's also home to different kinds of eagles, including the bald eagle, which is most often seen during the winter.

The great horned owl also lives in the Great Basin Desert. This large owl eats many different things, including small mammals and even other birds!

The great horned owl is sometimes called the "tiger owl." It's found in the Great Basin Desert and many other places across the United States.

Bugs are another common sight in the Great Basin. There are over 100 different kinds of butterflies in this region, and many different kinds of spiders can be found crawling over the rocks.

Scorpions are much like spiders, but they also have a stinger. A scorpion can cause a lot of pain when it stings someone! Some people are very afraid of scorpions, but they don't usually sting people. However, people should still be careful before picking up rocks that scorpions might live under.

Scorpions are most active after dark.
This means they're nocturnal.

Lots of Lizards!

Lizards are often found in dry environments, such as the Great Basin Desert. Some lizards in this region, such as the short-horned lizard and desert horned lizard, have **spines** that stick out of their heads like horns.

Other lizards, such as the Great Basin collared lizard, are known for the markings on their skin. This lizard has two black rings, or collars, and a white band around its neck. It's able to run quickly on just its two back legs once it sees its prey.

Short-horned lizards are just some of the many lizards that make their homes in the Great Basin Desert.

Mammals of the Great Basin Desert

coyote

badger

mountain lion

bighorn sheep

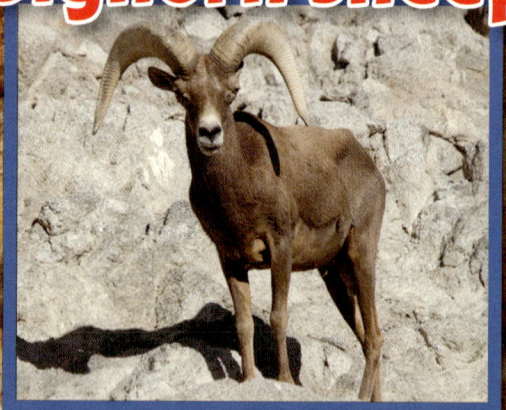

Glossary

adapt (uh-DAPT) To change to fit new conditions.

environment (ihn-VY-ruhn-muhnt) The natural world around us.

mammal (MA-muhl) Any warm-blooded animal whose babies drink milk from their mother's body and whose body is covered with hair or fur.

precipitation (prih-sih-puh-TAY-shun) Moisture that falls from the sky, including rain, snow, and ice.

region (REE-juhn) A broad area of land.

spine (SPYN) A long, sharp body part.

venom (VEH-nuhm) A poison produced by some animals.

Index

badger, 22

bald eagle, 16

bighorn sheep, 22

big sagebrush, 12

birds, 14, 16

bristlecone pine, 8, 10

butterflies, 18

coyote, 22

desert horned lizard, 20

Douglas fir, 10

Frémont, John C., 4

Great Basin collared lizard, 20

Great Basin rattlesnake, 14, 16

great horned owl, 16

limber pine trees, 10

lizards, 14, 20

mammals, 14, 16, 22

mountain lion, 22

scorpion(s), 18

short-horned lizard(s), 20

spiders, 18